OUTBACK COUNTRY

BY KIDS FROM CUNNAMULLA

INDIGENOUS LITERACY FOUNDATION™

MAP OF
D. Cansull
Bany
Bp
catch some feed.

CUNNAMULLA

Gun Club
Pony club
coffee shop
Race track
Emu
Kangaroo
N
NE
E
SE
S
SW
W
NW

CONTENTS

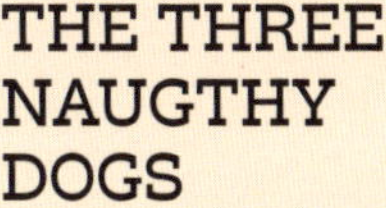

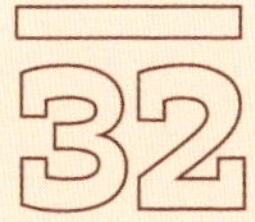

HosPital

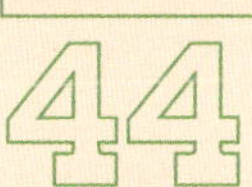

FOREWORD

As a Community member, I would like to highlight the importance of this well-put-together book. This book highlights the significance of literacy and education within our Community.

The book itself can serve as a promotional tool to connect generations within the Community – it may spark discussions about experiences, history and values that are crucial in preserving the Community's history. It may also be used as a tool to encourage other children to engage in reading and writing, fostering a culture of creativity and learning.

Witnessing the children write this book provided me with a sense of legacy. It signifies the continuation of storytelling traditions and the passing on of knowledge to the next generation. To say that I am proud of what the kids have achieved would be an understatement.

Well done to all involved.

Allen (Monk) Wharton, Cunnamulla Community member

The kids of Cunnamulla are something else – from the second they came into the room I knew they were going to make something special. Did we know what that something special was? No, not right away. This was the first workshop that I've had the honour of facilitating and I knew I didn't want to overproduce it. The kids know their stories and the town best, so I wanted to see the different ideas they would come up with. We wrote what felt like hundreds of stories to pick the ones you are about to read in this book. To the Cunnamulla kids, thank you for having me, thank you for sharing your stories and thank you for being you!

May your future be bright,

Bianca Hunt, ILF Ambassador

THE BANDY

BY MATTY RUSSELL

Cunnamulla is a little country town in South West Queensland. The Bandy is a paddock in Cunnamulla where you drive motorbikes – it's about two kilometres from town.

I love going to the Bandy because

it's my favourite thing in Australia to do.

There's no grass; it's just a big dirt patch.

I got one clutch bike, and I love clutches.

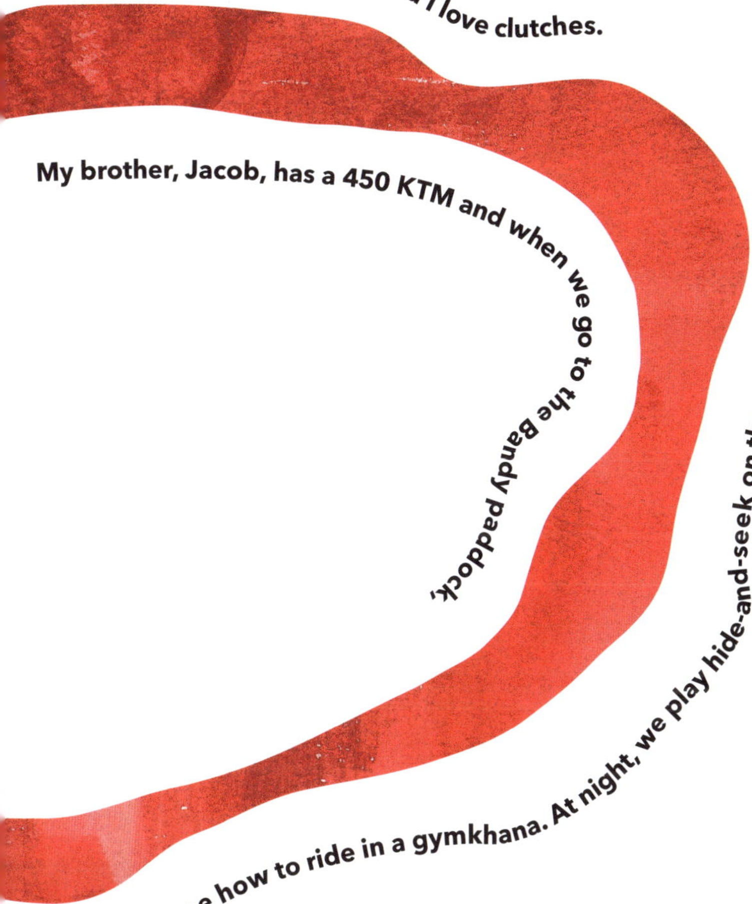

My brother, Jacob, has a 450 KTM and when we go to the Bandy paddock,

he teaches me how to ride in a gymkhana. At night, we play hide-and-seek on the motorbikes.

MAX AND ABIGAIL

By Emily Wharton

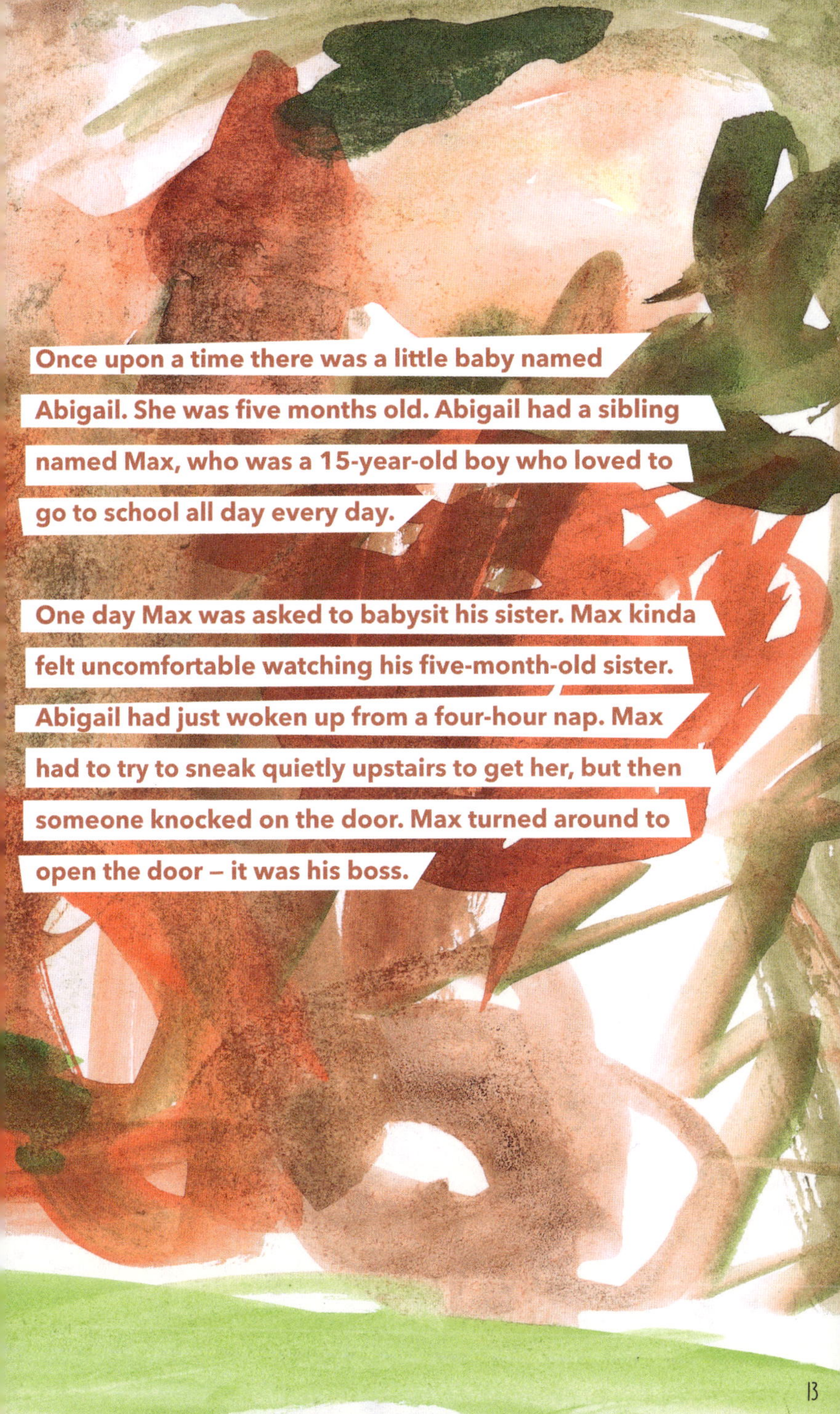

Once upon a time there was a little baby named Abigail. She was five months old. Abigail had a sibling named Max, who was a 15-year-old boy who loved to go to school all day every day.

One day Max was asked to babysit his sister. Max kinda felt uncomfortable watching his five-month-old sister. Abigail had just woken up from a four-hour nap. Max had to try to sneak quietly upstairs to get her, but then someone knocked on the door. Max turned around to open the door – it was his boss.

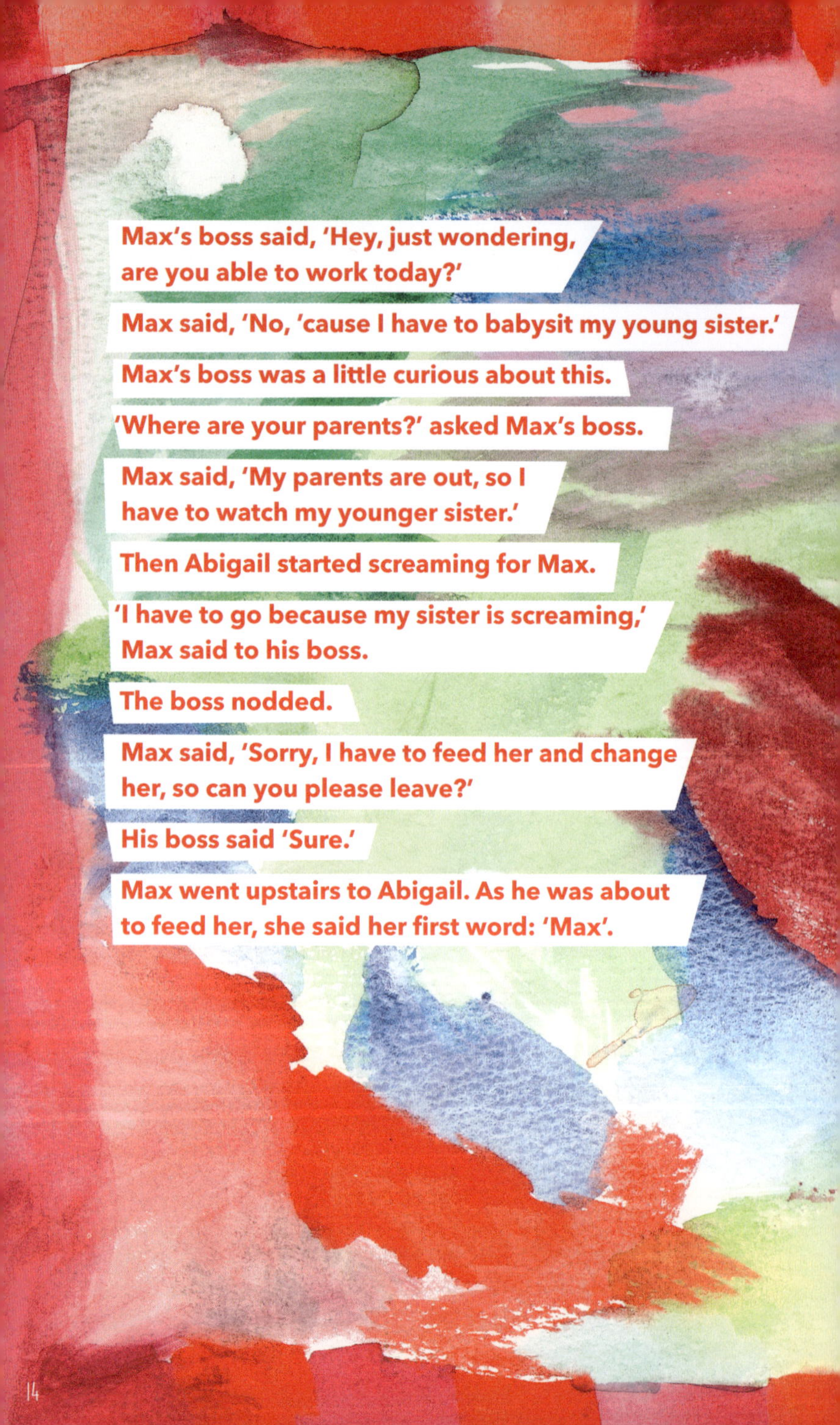

Max's boss said, 'Hey, just wondering, are you able to work today?'

Max said, 'No, 'cause I have to babysit my young sister.'

Max's boss was a little curious about this.

'Where are your parents?' asked Max's boss.

Max said, 'My parents are out, so I have to watch my younger sister.'

Then Abigail started screaming for Max.

'I have to go because my sister is screaming,' Max said to his boss.

The boss nodded.

Max said, 'Sorry, I have to feed her and change her, so can you please leave?'

His boss said 'Sure.'

Max went upstairs to Abigail. As he was about to feed her, she said her first word: 'Max'.

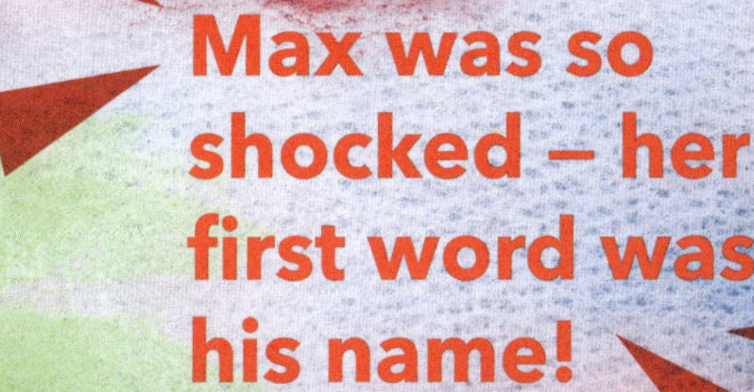

Max was so shocked – her first word was his name!

About thirty minutes later, their parents came home.

Abigail and Max were sleeping on the couch. They got woken up by their mum.

Max said, 'Mum, what time is it?'

Max's mum said, 'It's 10 pm.'

Max got up, had a shower and got ready for bed. As Max was getting into bed, his mum screamed in excitement.

Max ran downstairs to see what was wrong.

His mum said, 'Abigail was talking.'

Max said, 'Yeah! I know' and started walking back upstairs. His dad was so happy he had to post it on social media.

Godziller was minding his business and a sea beast came!

KONG AND GODZILLER

BY CARTER CAPEWELL

King Kong was up on the surface.
Then, some kids were disturbing Godziller.
Then, all of the titans came and they said,

'Do you want to fight?'

The kids said,

'Yes!'

All of them mashed together.

The big kids were up against the big titans, and the little kids were up against Suko.

All the villains started fighting the kids too.

Kong and Godziller were shocked.

Kong asked the villains a question.
He said, 'Why are you guys here?
I thought you didn't like us.'

Then, the villain said, 'What are you doing here?'

They all mashed together with a big cloud
of dust surrounding them.

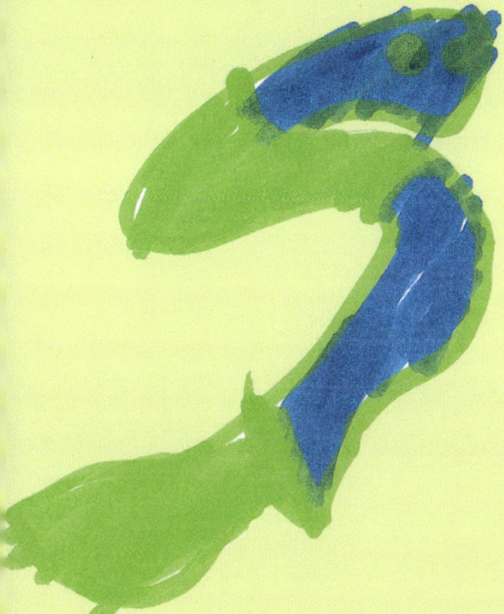

Then everyone became friends.

THE END

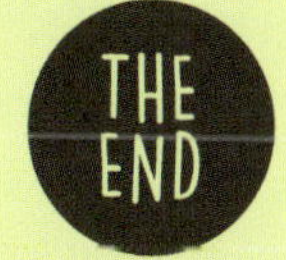

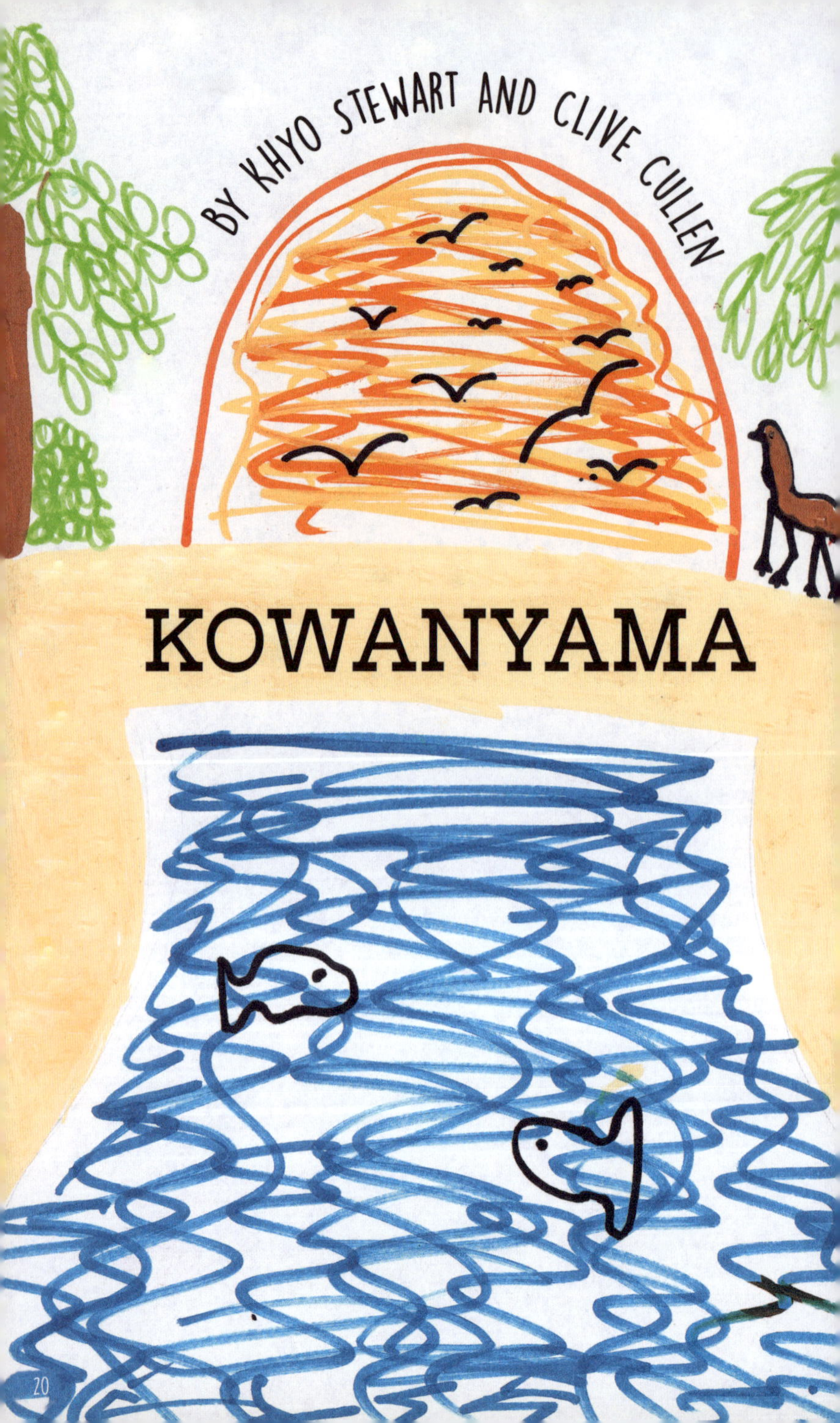

KOWANYAMA

BY KHYO STEWART AND CLIVE CULLEN

Once upon a time there were three kids in Kowanyama named Rashard, Kevin and John. They asked their mum to go out bush, but she said no.

When the sun started setting, they escaped into the bush to live there. When they got there they set up camp and went off hunting for food. But when they got back to camp, it was destroyed.

They set it back up, but by the time they finished it was night time. So they had to go to sleep.

When they woke up they saw a croc lurking at them.

The croc got closer and closer, then started sprinting at them.

They ran – the boys got out just in time.

Meanwhile, at home, Mum was worried sick about her kids.

Then, she heard the door slam shut and she went to look. She saw her three sons standing there.

She was very happy to see them and gave them all a big hug.

'Never run away again,' she told them.

They all lived happily ever after.

THE COLD AT THE HOT SPRINGS

BY MAGGIE-JO POWYER

Once upon a time there were two girls, Zoe Anderson and Claudia Kishi.

It was a very cold day so they went to the hot springs. The hot springs were right next to the weir and river walk. The river water is brown and there is an indoor swimming pool that was really warm.

It was so warm – actually, too warm – that they burnt themselves. They had to go jump into the indoor cold pool to cool down.

They were so happy that they didn't have to go to hospital, because if they had to go to hospital then they would have to get a needle.

Instead, they went to the weir to play on the rope swing. After that, they went to go get ice-cream.

After that, they went home to have a sleep.

THE END

OUTBACK

BY MACKENZIE PARANIHI

My name is Mackenzie. I am eleven years old, and I live in Cunnamulla with my mum, dad, and my brother, Tahi.

I often go to the weir for a swim. The weir is beautiful when it shines under the sun, but it can be dangerous because of the Moondagutta (Rainbow Serpent), who drags you under the water at night.

My cousin Starlett came over from Charleville to visit. We had so much fun then. You can catch so many yabbies at the lake. The lake is near Bourke Road and it's north of Cunnamulla. Me and my family caught so much fish in just one day.

COUNTRY

My pop Dulla is fun when he wants to be, and he loves celebrating our family's parties. When we visit the big tree, he gives us lollies. Pop Dulla is from Cunnamulla. My nan and pop met at a pub called Lynette's Pub, and they got together and had five kids: Brendan (the oldest), Aunty Tania, Diane, Ruffles and Michelle (the youngest).

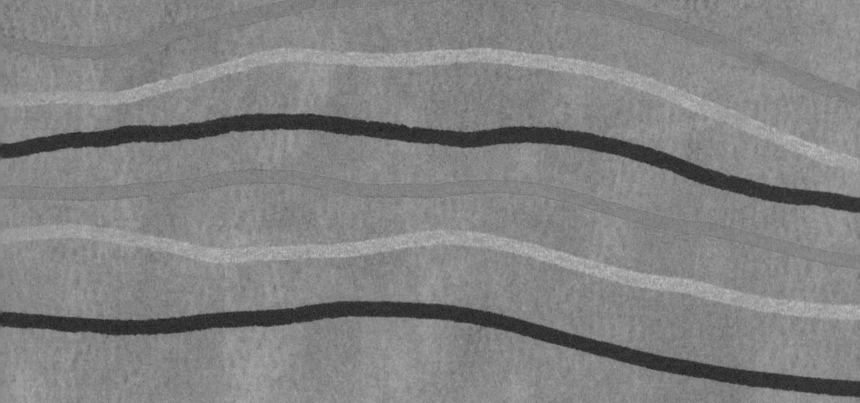

My nan Ruby lives in hospital. She wanted to put a picture of Jonathan Thurston on her wall, but the cleaners said she couldn't. Now, we are giving her photos to put on her wall – just small ones of her family members.

My uncle Cork is an Aboriginal fulla who lives in Cunnamulla. Uncle Cork sees us every time he walks around town. He calls me Kenzie and calls my brother Kiwi. Uncle Cork isn't from here – he's from the Top End. He's the sneakiest person in the world because whenever he sees us, he gives us lollies and money.

I have about 23 cousins! Their names are: Paulie, Blane, Tiane, Nathan, Cynthia, Ashton, Lawrance, Abby, Lexton, Antoinette, Jordy, Addison, Douglas, Djarwyn, Deston, Dominick, Mackenzie, Tahi, Starlett, Bernadette, Keith, Miari and Karmari.

My mum Michelle is 33 years old, and she has two kids named Mackenzie and Tahi. Tahi and I have a dad named Gully, and we think he is the best dad in the world.

One day, we went camping with Mum and Dad. We took the boat and kayaks for the weekend. Tahi and I love it here, and Mum and Dad always say that we have a lot of cousins – 23 in total! Aunty Tania is in her 30s, and she has five kids: Bernadette, Djarwyn, Douglas, Antoinette and Abby (the oldest). Abby graduated from Cunnamulla State School, where I go too.

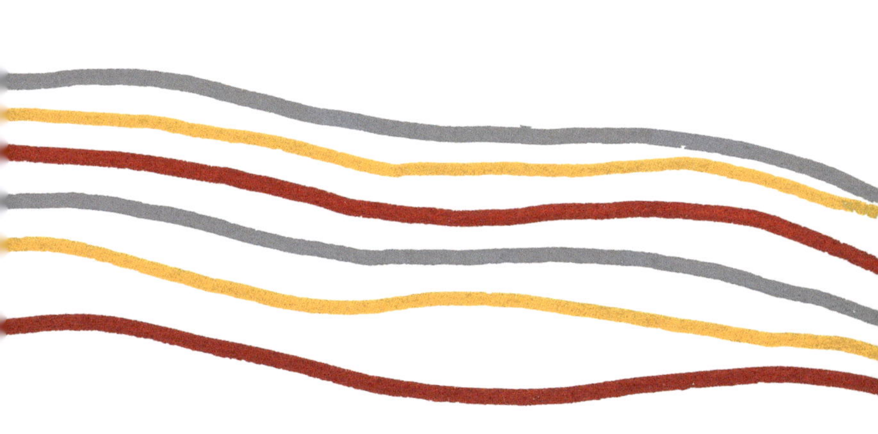

Aunty Diane is also in her 30s, and she has four kids: Starlett (my best friend in the whole world), Deston, Lexton and Ashton. Ashton is apparently the best in the family. Deston is kind when he wants to be and Lexton gives the best haircuts in the family.

Uncle Brendan is 42 years old, and he has three kids: Cynthia, Addison and Dominick. Cynthia is the most beautiful cousin in the world. Addison is an amazing horse rider, and soon she will be graduating from Cunnamulla State School. Dominick collects bottles and lids – he finds them fascinating.

THE THREE NAUGHTY DOGS

BY MYLEE RUSSELL

Ollie loves to play with his toys outside. He is a good dog, but he's a bit cheeky.

He gets up on the red table outside, steals the cat food and scatters it inside the house. Yesterday, he jumped off the back of my dad's car, and now he's limping on his left leg! He's very cheeky.

Worst of all, last year he pooped in my bed! I had to clean it up – he is very naughty and cheeky.

Herbie loves going for car rides. He enjoys playing in the water. He is a good dog, but he can be a bit of a terror.

He loves to play with Ollie and bite him. Whenever Ollie has a really long bone, Herbie steals it. When I act cheeky towards Herbie, he growls at me.

Patrick is my third dog. He loves to greet Dad when he comes home from roo shooting. He is a good dog, but when Dad washes the kangaroo blood off the car after shooting, Patrick loves to roll in it!

We have to give him a lot of baths when he does that.

All three of them love to snuggle up in my bed and sleep with me.

They are all naughty,

but I still love them.

THE WEIR

BY TAHI PARANIHI AND MATTY RUSSELL

Matty and Tahi went to the weir on a motorbike ride.

Tahi rode through one metre of water and caught a fish with his bare hands. Suddenly, his motorbike engine turned off – he couldn't turn it back on.

The bike wouldn't start, and the water was getting higher and higher.

Tahi tried to walk home, but he got stranded.

Matty stood on his bike, watching.

Matty said, 'Try to run more, and I'll come and pull you out.'

Matty had a saddlebag. He grabbed a rope and threw it to Tahi.

He pulled Tahi out, but the saddlebag snapped.

Then, Tahi passed out, and Matty had to do CPR.

Tahi woke up, and Matty took him back to town on the back of the bike.

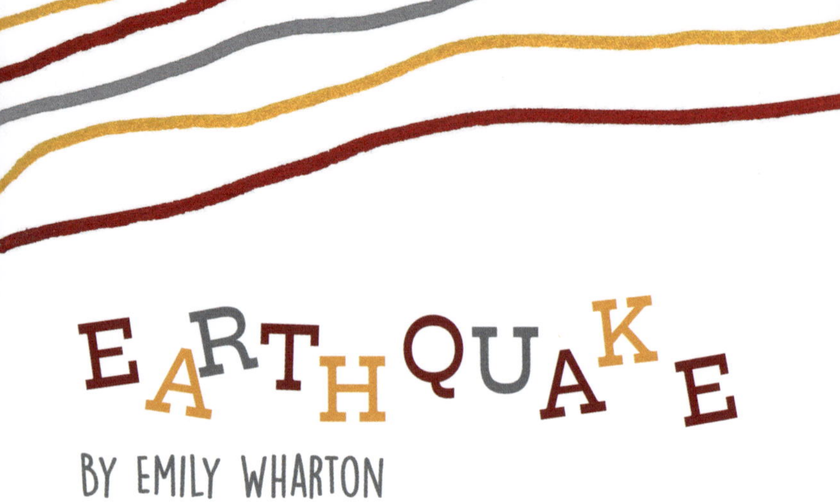

EARTHQUAKE

BY EMILY WHARTON

One day, at the Cunnamulla Hospital, there was a giant earthquake.

The hospital had over 100 patients, and they were stressed because they didn't know what was happening.

The nurses rushed around, checking to make sure everyone was okay.

There was an old lady who was about to turn 99 in a week. When a nurse went into her room, she realised the lady was missing.

The nurse quickly went to get the boss, who was curious about what was going on.

The boss and the nurse searched the hospital, making sure everything was okay. But the boss was very concerned about where the old lady had gone.

Then, the boss's work phone rang.

The boss answered – it was the lady's sister. The lady was very upset about everything that was happening.

The boss reassured her, saying, 'Try to keep her calm.'

Thirty minutes after the earthquake, the lady's sister brought her back to her room to help her settle down.

One hour later, the lady was calm – and it was all over.

THE SUPER

HORSE

BY MAGGIE-JO POWYER

One day, there was a superhero – and she was a horse named Montena.

Montena was 20 years old, and her owner's name was Maggie-Jo.

Their first adventure was to save the world from ending. The evil villain behind it all was Jack Frost.

First, he froze the world.

Then, he hit every country with rockets.

Finally, he forced everyone to leave their homes.

But Super Montena saved the day!

FISHING STORY

BY KHYO STEWART AND CLIVE CULLEN

One day, two boys named John and Kevin went fishing down at the Warrego River.

When they arrived, they saw that the river was flooded, but they didn't notice the sign that said: 'No Fishing Allowed'.

Then, the worst thing happened – (dramatic sound effects) – they fell in!

The current was strong, and they were flowing at 30 km/h.

Suddenly, they saw people running down to save them.

Someone stabbed a large stick into the ground and shouted, 'Hold onto it!'

John and Kevin grabbed the stick just in time and pulled themselves back to shore.

They were so happy to be safe!

But the most important lesson in this story is:

always check the signs before doing something!

BROKEN PHONE

BY MATTY RUSSELL

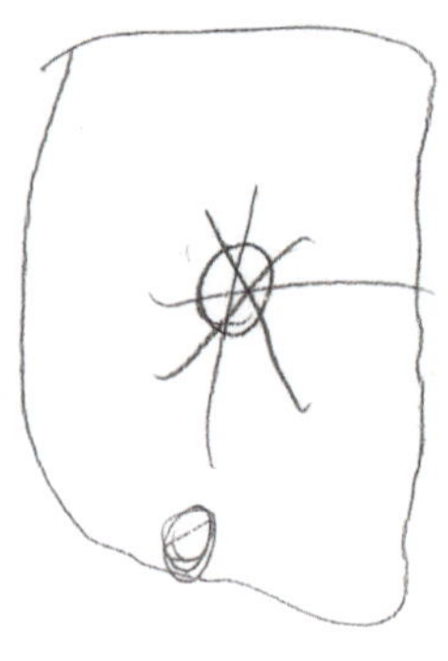

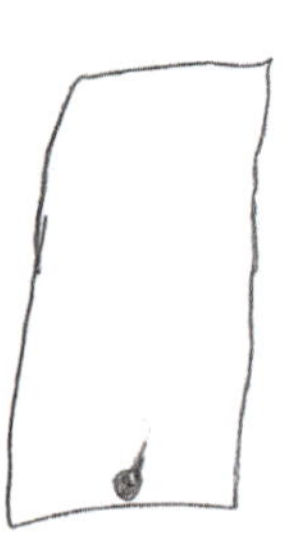

Once upon a time, Tahi and I went to the golf course to play a game of golf with Tahi's new golf clubs.

During the game, I accidentally smashed Tahi's phone with the club when I hit the golf ball!

After the game, I went home and bought Tahi a new phone using my IGA pay – the money I had been saving to buy a new golf set.

I was very cranky that I had to use all my savings from IGA.

The next morning, Tahi's new phone arrived, so I went to his house and dropped it off.

But then, Tahi told me he had already bought a new phone!

I was frustrated and started crying because I had wasted all my IGA savings for nothing.

Then, I thought for a minute ...

It was Valentine's Day the next day!

So, I got flowers and the phone ready to give to my girlfriend, Layla.

ACKNOWLEDGEMENTS

The Indigenous Literacy Foundation would like to thank all the wonderful people in Cunnamulla who helped in the creation of this book: the CACH team, Monk Wharton, Uncle Herb Wharton, Linda Wharton, the Deadly Choices team for helping out (particularly Jaz for letting us borrow her ute for a photoshoot) and staff at Cunnamulla Coffee Shop and the Warrego Hotel.

Shout out to Bianca Hunt for leading the workshop and inspiring the kids.

A special thank you to Tammy Hickey for being the project's greatest advocate and friend to all in Cunnamulla.

And most of all, to the wonderful Community of Cunnamulla, thank you for letting us come in and be a part of your story.

About the Indigenous Literacy Foundation

The Indigenous Literacy Foundation (ILF) is a national charity working with Aboriginal and Torres Strait Islander remote Communities across Australia. We are Community-led, responding to requests from remote Communities for culturally relevant books, including early learning board books, resources, and programs to support Communities to create and publish their stories in languages of their choice.

In 2024 the ILF won the Astrid Lindgren Memorial Award, given annually to a person or organisation for their outstanding contribution to children's or young adult literature.

First published in 2025 by the Indigenous Literacy Foundation
Gadigal Country
17/207 Kent Street
Sydney NSW 2000
ilf.org.au

Cataloging-in-Publication details are available from the National Library of Australia
www.trove.nla.gov.au

ISBN 9781923179585

Typesetting and design by Holly Doran
Printed in China by RR Donnelley Asia Printing Solutions Limited

CUNNAMULLA
FELLA